I0765875

Ferenc Margitics - Erika Figula - Zsuzsanna Pauwlik

Prevalence of School Bullying in Hungarian Primary and High Schools

Prevalence of School Bullying in Hungarian Primary and High Schools

Authored by:
Ferenc Margitics PhD.,Erika Figula PhD.,
Zsuzsanna Pauwlik PhD.
(margitics.ferenc@nye.hu)
Edited and published by: Ervin K. Kery
(publishing@kery.org)

ISBN: 9781699010594

CONTENTS

PREFACE

Our research group established by the Department of Psychology at the College of Nyíregyháza investigates the phenomena of school bullying and harassment. The term 'school bullying covers the behaviour where the aggressive act has no obvious cause (non-reactive aggression).

The aim of this present study is to reveal the structure of attitude- and behavior patterns that occur in the course of school bullying, the occurrence rate of the bully, the victim, the intervener participant, the helper participant and the bystander behavior patterns among primary students, in particular view of age and gender differences.

INTRODUCTION

The prevalence rate of school bullying show large variation depending on what are the influencing factors by the researchers; which period the measurement covers (e.g: last month, the previous six months, any time in the school years); what is the frequency that can be criterion in connection with bullying (eg once / twice in the period, once a month, once a week or more often), which definition is used (eg indirect or direct types) (Monks et al., 2009).

The research results show (Smith et al., 1999), that the victims of bullying are in minority (approximately 5-20% of the children and the harassers (who injured the others) are usually even less (about 2-20%).

Some students are also a harasser and a victim (attacker/victim); their prevalence rate is in connection with school bullying, beyond the above mentioned uncertainty, it changes a lot according to the applied methodology and criteria (Wolke et al., 2000).

According to Figula's (2004) domestic test, in school situations the rate of victims is 26, 1%, the rate of harassers is 12,9°%, the rate of aggressive/victims is 26,5%.

In childhood and adolescence, aggression is often described as a stable characteristic. Other researches show that bullying has a different process (Farrington, 1991; Goldstein, 1994; Loeber & Stouthamer-Loeber, 1998).

In fact, the increase and peak of bullying can be in the years of adolescence while during the high school years it shows a declining tendency. (Nansel et al., 2001; Pellegrini & Bartini, 2001).

With age the incidence tendency of bullying moves from physical aggression toward indirect and covert aggression. There are more boys in the category of offenders, while among the victims there is balance between the genders. Physical maltreatment is typical of boys, covert and indirect harassment is typical of girls (Olweus, 1993; Smith et al., 1999).

According to the researchers of bullying, there is connection between family atmosphere and aggressive behavior. It is likely that those children who find aggressive behavior useful it is typical that conflict is often present in their family, they take part in bullying at home and in aggressive behavior, and they feel that aggression has a functional value to achieve their goals. Surely they learn these behaviors at home and it is likely that the learned things at home are practiced at school by them (Espelage & Swearer, 2003).

The role of family in the development of bullying has been examined by several researches. Researchers have found strong links between the aggressive behavior of young people and the lack of family cohesion (Gorman-Smith et al., 1996), inadequate family control (Farrington, 1991), family bullying (Thornberry, 1994), belligerence (Loeber & Dishion, 1983) and poor problem-solving skills (Tolan et al., 1986).

Furthermore, the presence of family conflicts and parental problems also show close contact with aggression in childhood (Henggeler et al., 1998).

More researchers have revealed connection among parental educational style, family atmosphere and school bullying. For example, according to Olweus' Scandinavian Youth Research (1980, 1993) he concluded that the violent boys' families can be often characterized by the lack of coziness, the use of physical bullying within the family and the inability to control extra-curricular activities.

The above findings in Bowers, Smith and Binney's research (1994) were supplemented by that the harassers' family members have high claim to power. About the families of the victims it turned out that the family is very cohesive and probably the mother is overprotective (Berdondini & Smith, 1996).

The researches examining the proactive victim's family background revealed that the harsh, negative parental behavior is quite common in the proactive victims' families; the parents are often unable to control their emotions. The proactive boy victims often have close relationship with their mother but their relationship is distant with their father. The proactive girl victims' mother is rather hostile than overprotective (Révész, 2007).

The aim of this present study is to reveal the structure of the aggressive attitude – and behavior patterns in school practice, the occurrence rate of the bully, the victim, the intervener participant, the helper participant and the bystander behavior patterns among primary and high school students, in particular view of age and gender differences.

METHODOLOGY

Participants

In the study 1365 (731 girls, 634 boys) primary and high school students took part.

The distribution of the sample in terms of school types is as follows:

- ➢ Primary schools: 856 people (410 girls and 441 boys)
- ➢ High schools: 460 people (308 girls and 152 boys)

We examined the following age groups:

- ➢ 11-12 years: 410 individuals (205 girls and 205 boys)
- ➢ 13-14 years: 446 individuals (205 girls and 241 boys)
- ➢ 15-16 years: 259 individuals (153 girls and 106 boys)
- ➢ 17-19 years: 250 individuals (165 girls and 85 boys)

Measures

The Examination of School Bullying

The Questionnaire on School Bullying (Figula et al., 2019).

For purposes of identifying patterns of behaviour in school bullying, the School Bullying Questionnaire was used.

The 70 items of SBQ offers options of "almost never," "sometimes," "often," "almost always," and investigates the phenomena of school bullying and abuse in everyday life through five dimensions.

With the exception of "ally intervener" scale, all dimensions include further subscales. (Chart 1).

Chart 1. Scales and Subscales of the School Bullying Questionnaire

Scales and Subscales	Item	Cronbach-alfa
Victim Scale	**33**	**0,847**
Cognitive Subscale (Conscious recognition of abuse and processing it)	15	0,877
Affective Subscale (The emotional effect of abuse)	12	0,864
Somatic reaction (Somatic reaction to abuse / acting out)	3	0,758
Lack of Social Support Subscale (Lack of acceptance in class community)	3	0,814
Ally Intervener Scale	**3**	**0,784**
Rescuer Intervener Scale	**8**	**0,753**
Intervening to Pacify Subscale	3	0,748

Intervening to Ask for Help Subscale	2	0,778
Affective Subscale (Inner tension as a result of witnessing aggression)	3	0,749
Bystander Scale	**9**	**0,768**
Keeping Distance Subscale	6	0,758
Fear Subscale	3	0,743
Bully Scale	**17**	**0,843**
Physical Aggression Subscale	4	0,845
Verbal Aggression Subscale	5	0,849
Exclusion Subscale	5	0,754
Advantage From Attack Subscale	3	0,768

RESULTS

Comparing the scales and subscales of Questionnaire on School Bullying with each other, we calculated the average of values to a given statement within the tested scales and subscales.

In school practice we examined the structural characteristics of attitude and behavior patterns in connection with school bullying according to age groups (11-12 year olds, 13-14 year olds, 15-16 year olds, and 17-19 year olds).   Within age groups we examined separately the structural characteristics of the behavior patterns of genders.

11-12 year old age group

Figure 1 shows the structure of behavior patterns in connection with school bullying in the 11-12 year old age group.

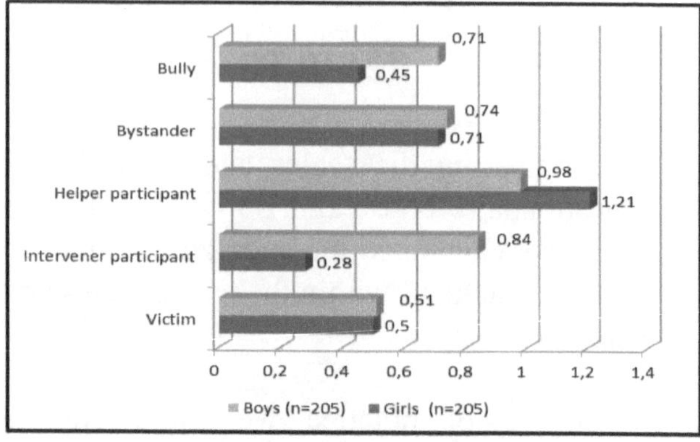

Figure 1. The structure of behavior patterns in connection with school bullying in the 11-12 year old age group

The figure shows that there are differences between the girls and the boys in the structure of behavior patterns in connection with school bullying. In this age group helper participant was typical of boys then intervener participant was the next. It was followed by bystander and bully behavior patterns. Victim behavior pattern was the least typical of boys.

In case of the girls, from the behavior patterns of school bullying helper participant was the most dominant and it was followed by bystander behavior pattern. Next time there were victim and bully behavior patterns. Intervener participant was the least typical of girls.

We also examined the components (subscales) of the behavior patterns (scales) in connection with school bullying in this age group.

Figure 2 shows the structure of the components of bully behavior pattern.

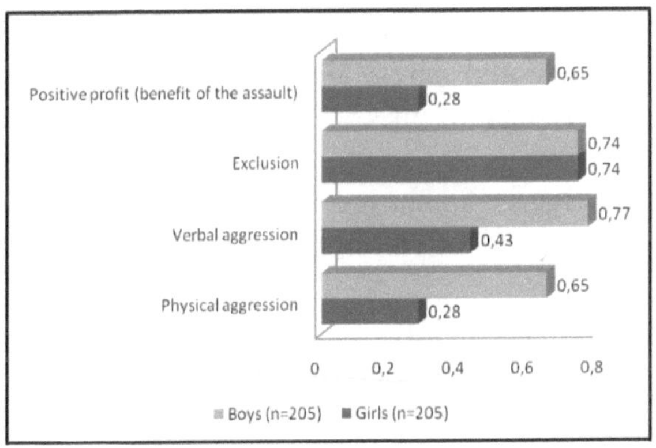

Figure 2. The structure of the components of bully behavior pattern in the 11-12 year old age group

In this age group there was a difference between the boys and the girls in the structure of bully behavior pattern. The aggressive behavior patterns of the boys were characterized by verbal aggression and willingness for the exclusion of others; it was followed by positive profit (benefit of the assault). Physical aggression was the least typical of them.

In case of the girls, the most dominant component of bully behavior pattern was exclusion, which was followed by verbal aggression. Positive profit (benefit of the assault) and physical aggression were not very typical of girls.

Figure 3 shows the structure of the components of victim behavior pattern.

In the structure of victim behavior pattern, we do not find significant gender differences. In case of both genders, social support (refusal in the class community) was the main component of becoming a victim, in the case of girls, it was followed by affective behavior pattern (emotional effect of the insult), and in case of the boys it was followed by cognitive behavior pattern (apperception and assimilation of the insult).

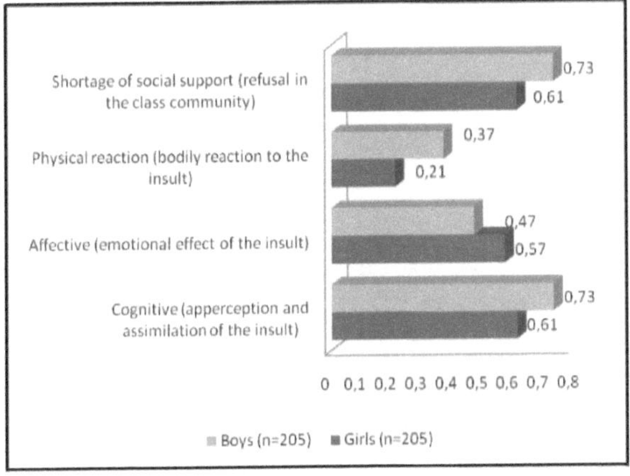

Figure 3. The structure of the components of victim behavior pattern in the 11-12 year old age group

In the third place we found cognitive behavior pattern (apperception and assimilation of the insult) in case of the girls and affective behavior pattern (emotional effect of the insult) in case of the boys. Physical reaction (bodily reaction to the insult) was the least typical of both genders.

Figure 4 shows the structure of the components of helper participant behavior pattern.

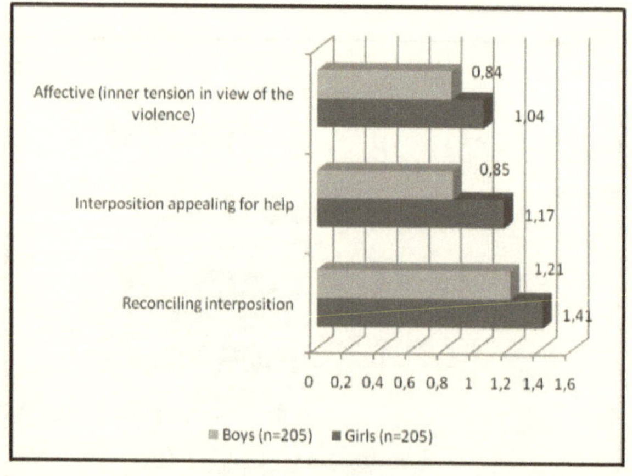

Figure 4. The structure of the components of helper participant behavior pattern in the 11-12 year old age group

In this age group helper participant behavior pattern showed similar structure in case of both genders. In the case of both genders, reconciling interposition was the most typical and it was followed by interposition appealing for help. In this age group, affective behavior pattern (inner tension in view of the violence) was the least typical.

Figure 5 shows the structure of the components of bystander behavior pattern.

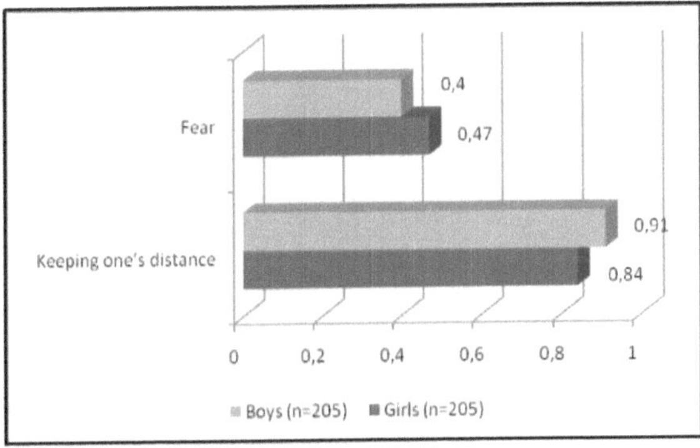

Figure 5. The structure of the components of bystander behavior pattern in the 11-12 year old age group

We did not find significant gender differences in the structure of bystander behavior pattern. In case of both genders, bystander behavior pattern was characterized by the effort of keeping one's distance, it was followed by fear.

13-14 year old age group

Figure 6 shows the structure of behavior patterns in connection with school bullying in the 13-14 year old age group.

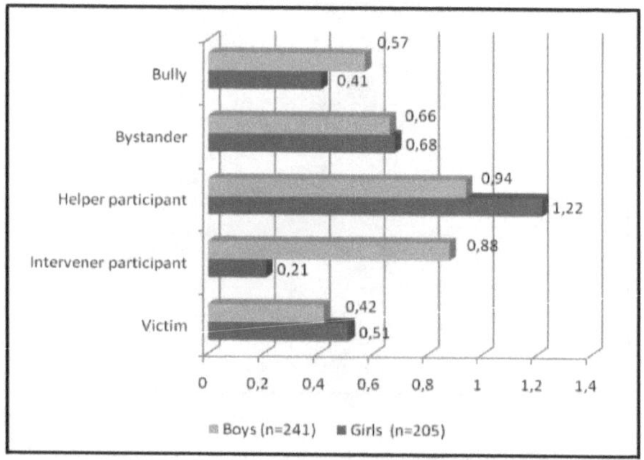

Figure 6. The structure of behavior patterns in connection with school bullying in the 13-14 year old age group.

The figure shows that in the 13-14 year old age group there was not significant change in the structure of the behavior patterns in connection with school bullying compared to the other age group.

In this age group, helper participant was also the most typical of boys and it was followed by intervener participant. Finally it was followed by bystander and bully behavior patterns. Victim behavior pattern was the least typical of boys.

In case of the girls, from the behavior patterns of school bullying helper participant was also the most dominant in this age group and it was followed by bystander behavior pattern. Next time there were victim and bully behavior patterns. Intervener participant was the least typical of girls.

We also examined the components (subscales) of the behavior patterns (scales) in connection with school bullying in this age group.

Figure 7 shows the structure of the components of bully behavior pattern.

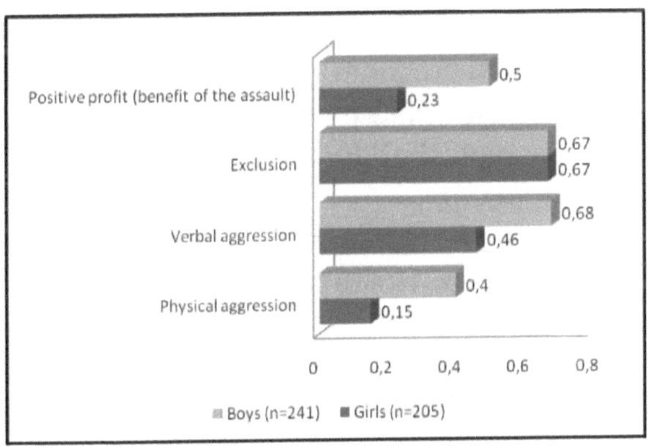

Figure 7. The structure of the components of bully behavior pattern at 13-14 year old age group

In the 13-14 year old age group there were not significant changes compared to the previous age group in the structure of bully behavior pattern.

In this age group similarly to the previous age group there was a difference between the boys and the girls in the structure of bully behavior pattern. The aggressive behavior patterns of the boys were characterized by verbal aggression and willingness for the exclusion of others; it was followed by positive profit (benefit of the assault). Physical aggression was the least typical of them. In case of the girls, the most dominant component of bully behavior pattern was exclusion, which was followed by verbal aggression. Positive profit (benefit of the assault) and physical aggression were not very typical of girls.

Figure 8 shows the structure of the components of victim behavior pattern.

In the 13-14 year old age group, we do not find significant changes in the structure of victim behavior pattern compared to the previous group. In case of both genders, social support (refusal in the class community) was also the main component of becoming a victim, in case of the girls, it was followed by affective behavior pattern (emotional effect of the insult), and in case of the boys it was followed by cognitive behavior pattern (apperception and assimilation of the insult).

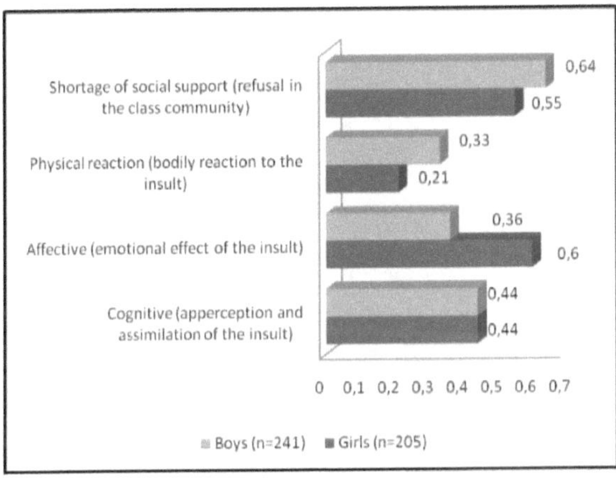

Figure 8. The structure of the components of victim behavior pattern in the 13-14 year old age group

In the third place we found cognitive behavior pattern (apperception and assimilation of the insult) in case of the girls and affective behavior pattern (emotional effect of the insult) in case of the boys. Physical reaction (bodily reaction to the insult) was the least typical of both genders.

Figure 9 shows the structure of the components of helper participant behavior pattern.

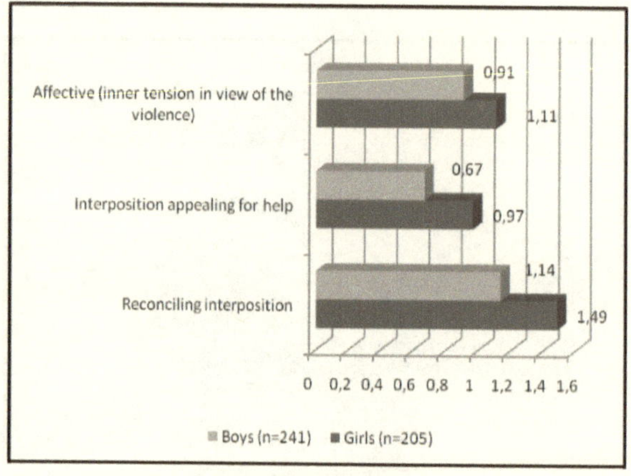

Figure 9. The structure of the components of helper participant behavior pattern in the 13-14 year old age group

In this age group helper participant behavior pattern also showed similar structure in case of both genders. From the components of helper participant in the 13-14 old age group – compared to the previous age group- reconciling interposition was also the most frequent behavior pattern. Contrary to the previous age group, it was followed by affective behavior pattern (inner tension in view of the violence) and finally helper participant came after it (in case of the previous age group, helper participant was the second most typical behavior pattern.

Figure 10 shows the structure of the components of bystander behavior pattern.

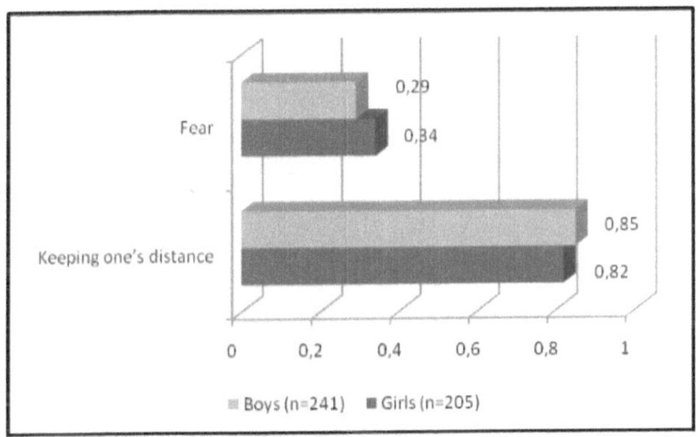

Figure 10. The structure of the components of bystander behavior pattern in the 13-14 year old age group

In this age group we did not find significant gender differences in the structure of bystander behavior pattern either. In case of both genders- similarly to the previous age group- bystander behavior pattern was characterized by the effort of keeping one's distance, it was followed by fear.

15-16 year old age group

Figure 11 shows the structure of behavior patterns in connection with school bullying in the 15-16 year old age group.

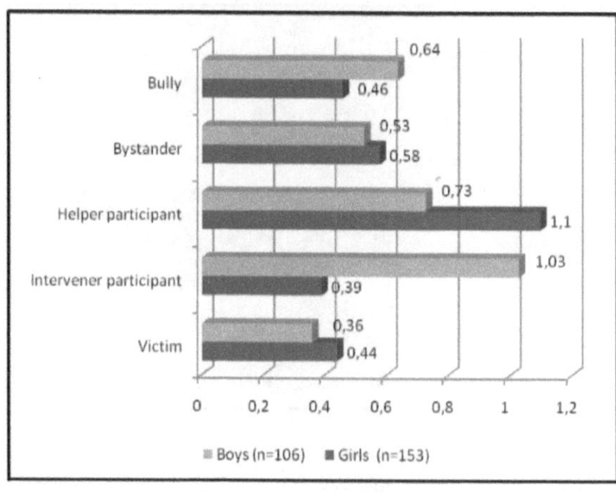

Figure 11. The structure of behavior patterns in connection with school bullying in the 15-16 year old age group

In the 15-16 year old age group the structure of the behavior patterns in connection with school bullying do not show significant changes compared to the previous age group in case of the girls. In this age group we found helper participant the most dominant reaction; it was followed by bystander behavior pattern. Then victim and bully behavior patterns approximately at the same level came after it. In case of the girls, here also intervener participant was the least typical.

In the 15-16 year old age group the structure of behavior patterns in connection with school bullying shows changes in case of the boys compared to the previous age group. In case of the boys, the most dominant behavior pattern was intervener participant and it was followed by helper participant. Then bully and bystander behavior patterns came after them. In this age group, victim behavior pattern was also the least typical of boys.

Figure 12 shows the structure of the components of bully behavior pattern.

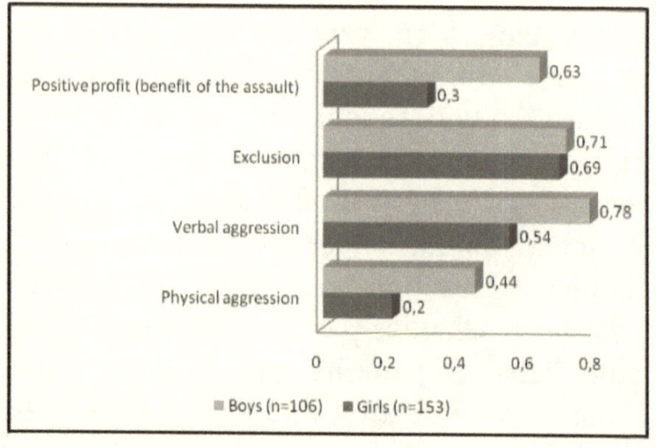

Figure 12. The structure of the components of bully behavior pattern in the 15-16 year old age group

In the 15-16 year old age group there were not significant changes compared to the previous age group in the structure of bully behavior pattern.

In this age group similarly to the previous age group there was a difference between the boys and the girls in the structure of bully behavior pattern. The aggressive behavior patterns of the boys were characterized by verbal aggression and willingness for the exclusion of others; it was followed by positive profit (benefit of the assault). Physical aggression was the least typical of them. In case of the girls, the most dominant component of bully behavior pattern was also exclusion, which was followed by verbal aggression. Positive profit (benefit of the assault) and physical aggression were not very typical of girls.

Figure 13 shows the structure of the components of victim behavior pattern.

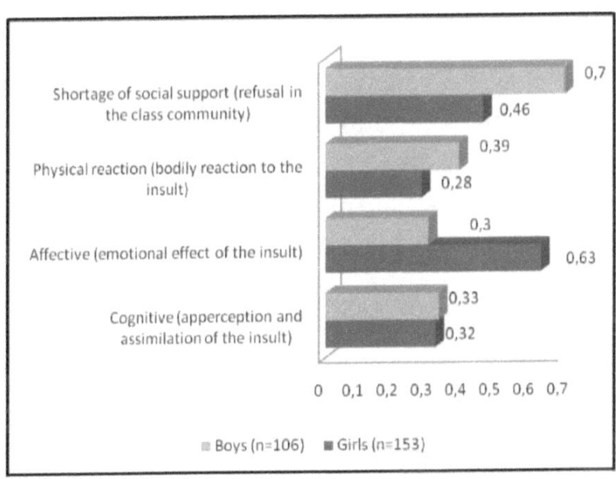

Figure 13. The structure of the components of victim behavior pattern in the 15-16 year old age group

In the 15-16 year old age group, changes

occurred in the structure of victim behavior pattern compared to the previous age group. From this age we find significant gender differences in the structure of victim behavior pattern. In case of the girls, affective (emotional effect of the insult) came into the first place, which was followed by social support (refusal in the class community) and cognitive (apperception and assimilation of the insult).

Physical reaction (bodily reaction to the insult) was the least typical of girls. In case of the boys, social support (refusal in the class community) was the most dominant component of victim behavior pattern, which was followed by physical reaction (bodily reaction to the insult) and cognitive (apperception and assimilation of the insult). Affective reaction (emotional effect of the insult) was the least typical of boys.

Figure 14 shows the structure of the components of helper participant behavior pattern.

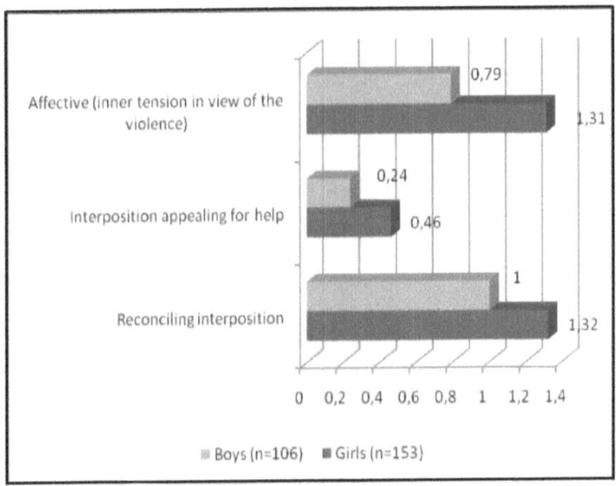

Figure 14. The structure of the components of helper participant behavior pattern in the 15-16 year old age group

In this age group helper participant behavior pattern showed similar structure in case of both genders. In the 15-16 year old age group from the components of helper participant– similarly to the previous age group- reconciling interposition was the most typical behavior pattern. It was followed by affective (inner tension in view of the violence) (in case of the girls it was at the same level with reconciling interposition. Finally, helper participant came after them.

Figure 15 shows the structure of the components of bystander behavior pattern.

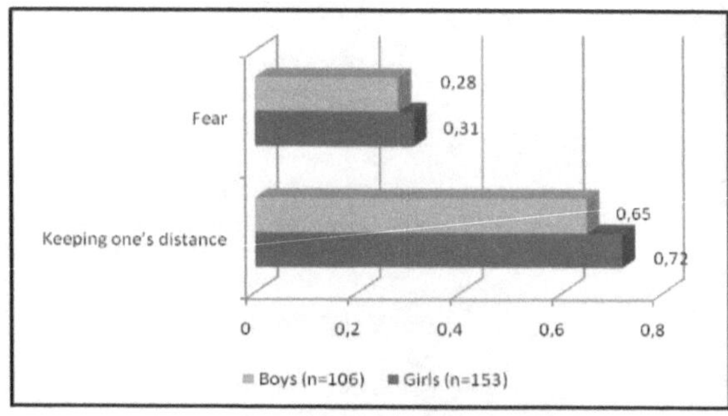

Figure 15. The structure of the components of bystander behavior pattern in the 15-16 year old age group

In this age group we did not find significant gender differences in the structure of bystander behavior pattern either. In case of both genders- similarly to the previous age group- bystander behavior pattern was characterized by the effort of keeping one's distance, it was followed by fear.

17-19 year old age group

Figure 16 shows the structure of behavior patterns in connection with school bullying in the 17-19 year old age group.

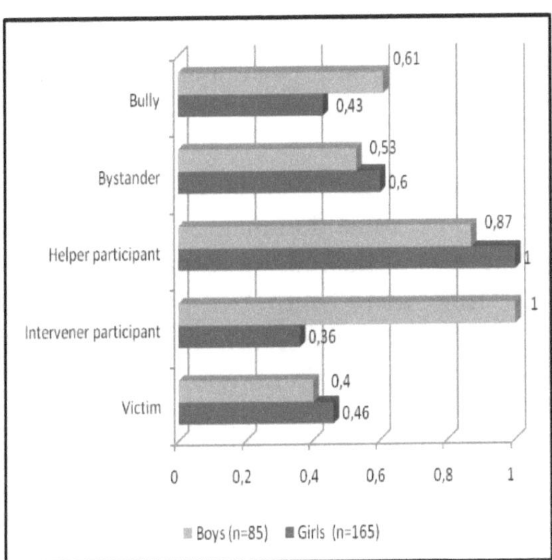

Figure 16. The structure of behavior patterns in connection with school bullying in the 17-19 year old age group.

The figure shows that in the 17-19 year old age group there were not significant changes in the structure of the behavior patterns in connection with school bullying compared to the other age group.

In this age group, helper participant was

also the most typical of girls and it was followed by bystander behavior pattern. It was followed by victim and bully behavior patterns. Intervener participant was the least typical of the girls.

In case of the boys, intervener participant was also the most dominant in this age group and it was followed by helper participant. Next time there were bystander and bully behavior patterns. Victim behavior pattern was the least typical of boys.

Figure 17 shows the structure of the components of bully behavior pattern.

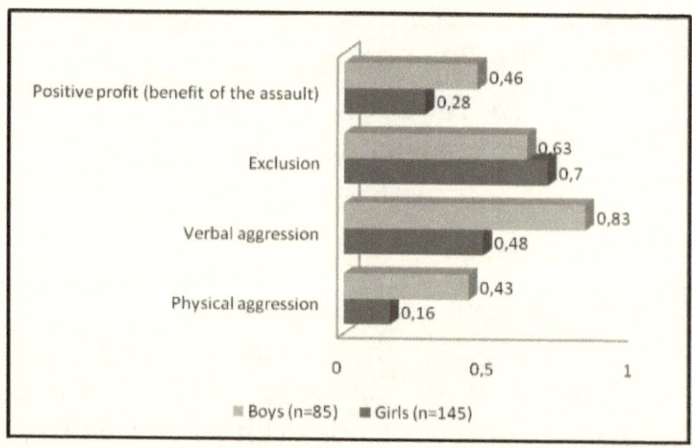

Figure 17. The structure of the components of bully behavior pattern in the 17-19 year old age group

In the 17-19 year old age group there were not significant changes compared to the previous age group in the structure of bully behavior pattern.

In this age group -similarly to the previous age group- there was a difference between the boys and the girls in the structure of bully behavior pattern. The aggressive behavior patterns of the boys were characterized by verbal aggression and willingness for the exclusion of others; it was followed by positive profit (benefit of the assault). Physical aggression was the least typical of them.

In case of the girls, the most dominant component of bully behavior pattern was also exclusion, which was followed by verbal aggression. Positive profit (benefit of the assault) and physical aggression were not very typical of girls.

Figure 18 shows the structure of the components of victim behavior pattern.

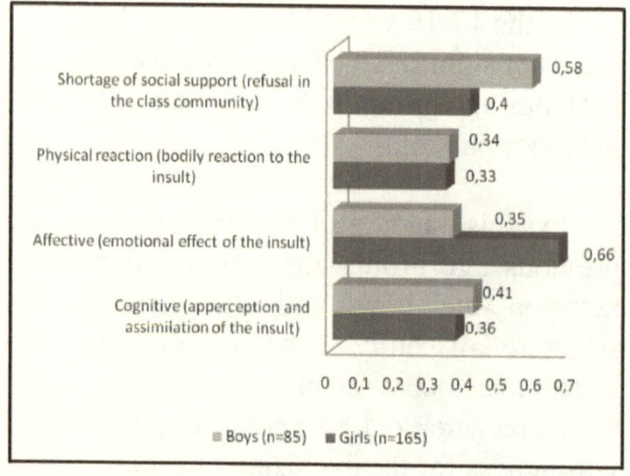

Figure 18. The structure of the components of victim behavior pattern in the 17-19 year old age group

In the 17-19 year old age group, changes did not occur in the structure of victim behavior pattern compared to the previous age group. In case of the girls, affective (emotional effect of the insult) stayed at the first place, which was followed approximately equally by social support (refusal in the class community), cognitive reaction (apperception and assimilation of the insult) and physical reaction (bodily reaction to the insult).

In case of the boys, social support (refusal in the class community) was also the most dominant component of victim behavior pattern, which was followed by cognitive reaction (apperception and assimilation of the insult). Physical reaction (bodily reaction to the insult) and affective reaction (emotional effect of the insult) were the least typical of the boys.

Figure 19 shows the structure of the components of helper participant behavior pattern.

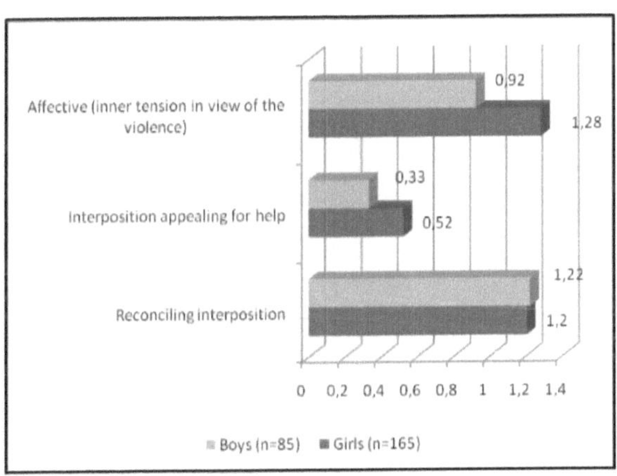

Figure 19. The structure of the components of helper participant behavior pattern in the 17-19 year old age group

In this age group helper participant behavior pattern showed similar structure in case of both genders. In the 17-19 year old age group from the components of helper participant – similarly to the previous age group- reconciling interposition was also the most typical behavior pattern of the boys. It was followed by affective reaction (inner tension in view of the violence) behavior pattern in case of the boys. In the case of girls the order was reverse, affective reaction (inner tension in view of the violence) came into the first place, reconciling interposition came after it. In case of both genders, helper participant was the next.

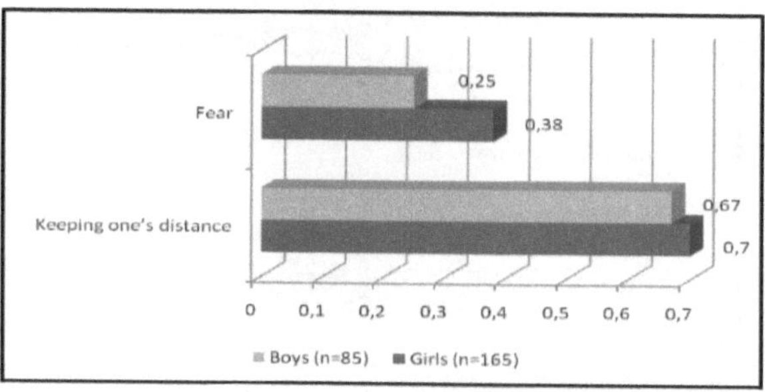

Figure 20. The structure of the components of bystander behavior pattern in the 17-19 year old age group

Figure 20 shows the structure of the components of bystander behavior pattern.

In this age group we did not find significant gender differences in the structure of bystander behavior pattern either. In case of both genders- similarly to the previous age group- bystander behavior pattern was characterized by the effort of keeping one's distance, it was followed by fear.

Analysis of Gender Differences

We also examined in reference to the scales and subscales of the Questionnaire on School Bullying – according to the individual age groups-whether there are significant differences between the genders.

Chart 2. shows the gender differences between the individual components of bully behavior pattern.

Examining the individual components of bully behavior pattern, we found that in all age groups physical aggression, verbal aggression and positive profit (benefit of the assault) were more significantly typical of boys. In case of exclusion, we did not find significant gender differences.

Chart. 2. The extent of gender differences in the individual subscales of Bully Scale (p<)

Subscale of Bully Scale	11-12 years	13-14-years	15-16 years	17-19 years
Physical aggression	0,002	0,000	0,004	0,000
Verbal aggression	0,000	0,000	0,018	0,000
Exclusion	0,468	0,917	0,861	0,482
Positive profit (benefit of the assault)	0,000	0,000	0,000	0,048

Chart 3 shows the gender differences between the individual components of victim behavior pattern.

Examining the components of victim behavior pattern, there was a different situation. In all age groups, we find significant differences in point of affective (emotional effect of the insult), the girls were more liable to it than the boys.

Chart 3. The extent of gender differences in the individual subscales of Victim Scale (p<)

Subscale of Victim Scale	11-12 years	13-14 years	15-16 years	17-19 years
Cognitive (apperception and assimilation of the insult)	0,274	0,941	0,873	0,308
Affective (emotional effect of the insult)	**0,050**	**0,000**	**0,000**	**0,000**
Physical reaction (bodily reaction to the insult)	**0,005**	**0,019**	0,128	0,888
Shortage of social support (refusal in the class community)	0,076	0,159	**0,017**	0,385

The boy students in primary school as victims were more liable to physical reaction (bodily reaction to the insult) than the girls. This kind of inclination also characterized the boys much more in high school but at this age the difference was not so significant.

Social support (refusal in the class community) was also more typical of boys but this difference was only significant at the age of 15-16. We could not demonstrate significant difference in case of cognitive (apperception and assimilation of the insult).

Chart 4 shows the gender differences between the individual components of helper participant.

Examining the individual components of helper participant we found that in all age groups affective reaction (inner tension in view of the violence) was significantly more typical of girls than boys. Primary school girls and girls at the age of 15-16 were also more liable to reconciling interposition and interposition appealing for help.

Chart 4. The extent of gender differences in the individual subscales of Helper Participant Scale (p<)

Subscale of Helper participant Scale	11-12 years	13-14-years	15-16 years	17-19 years
Reconciling interposition	**0,011**	**0,000**	**0,013**	0,851
Interposition appealing for help	**0,000**	**0,000**	**0,018**	0,076
Affective (inner tension in view of the violence)	**0,004**	**0,004**	**0,000**	**0,001**

Examining the individual components of bystander behavior pattern, we found that fear in all age groups was more typical of girls than boys. Keeping one's distance was typical of boys in primary school; it was typical of girls in high school. In all age groups, gender differences were not significant neither in case of fear nor in case of keeping one's distance.

DISCUSSION

The aim of this present study was to reveal the structure of the aggressive attitude – and behavior patterns in school practice, the occurrence rate of the bully, the victim, the intervener participant , the helper participant and the bystander behavior patterns among primary and high school students, in particular view of gender and age differences.

In case of the primary school students (11-14 year olds) from the reactions on school bullying the most frequent behavior pattern – without reference to genders - was helper participant. Helper participant primarily meant reconciling interposition, which was followed by interposition appealing for help in the age group of 11-12 year old students and it became the least preferred behavior pattern in the age group of 13-14 year old students. While affective (inner tension in view of the violence) was the weakest component of helper participant in the age group of 11-12 year old students, it was a more dominant tendency than interposition appealing for help from parents in the age group of 13-14 year old students.

In case of the high school students, in point of the strongest reactions on school bullying, we find differences between the boys and the girls. In the case of girls – similarly to the primary school students-interposition appealing for help remained the most dominant behavior pattern, in which reconciling interposition, affective (inner tension in view of the violence) and interposition appealing for help were the order.

Examining helper participant behavior pattern, we found that effort for helper participant was significantly more typical of girls than boys in all age groups. Within helper participant behavior pattern, affective reaction (inner tension in view of the violence) was significantly more typical of girls than boys. Primary school girls and 15-16 year old girls were also more liable to reconciling interposition and interposition appealing for help than the boys at the same age. In case of the boys, from high school age groups intervener participant behavior pattern become the most dominant from the reactions on school bullying.

Examining intervener participant behavior pattern, we find that intervener participant was significantly more typical of boys than girls in all age groups. In case of the girls, this behavior pattern was the least used reaction in all age groups.

We also find significant differences between the boys and the girls in point of the second most dominant behavior pattern of school bullying. In case of the girls of all age groups, it was bystander behavior pattern, from the components of which keeping one's distance was more determining than fear (However, fear was more typical of girls than boys in all age groups).

We found bystander behavior pattern less typical of boys, in case of the primary school students it was the third, in case of the high school students it was the fourth most dominant behavior pattern, from the components of which keeping one's distance was also the most dominant in the case of boys.

In case of the primary school boys, intervener participant was the second most dominant behavior pattern, in case of the high school boys, it was helper participant, from the components of which reconciling interposition was the most important, and it was followed by affective reaction (inner tension in view of the violence). From the components of helper participant-interposition appealing for help from adults was the least typical of boys (this tendency from the age of 13 without reference to genders was the least preferred component of helper participant behavior pattern.

Bully behavior pattern on school bullying was not typical of either of the groups. We demonstrated that bully behavior pattern was significantly more typical of boys than girls in all age groups. In case of the boys of all age groups, physical aggression, verbal aggression and positive profit (benefit of the assault) were significantly more typical. In case of exclusion, we did not find important differences between the genders.

From the reactions on school bullying, victim behavior pattern was the least typical of the sample. At the age of 11-12, both the girls and the boys became victims of school bullying approximately at the same level. From the age of 13-14, we found this behavior pattern more typical of girls, which was not significant in the case of either of the age groups.

Examining the individual components of victim behavior pattern, the situation was different. In case of affective reaction (emotional effect of the insult) we find significant differences in all age groups, the girls seem to be more liable to it than the boys.

The primary school boys seemed to be more liable to physical reaction (bodily reaction to the insult) than the girls. This kind of inclination was more typical of the high school boys but at this age, it was not so significant.

Claim for social support (refusal in the class community) was also more typical of boys but this difference was significant in case of 15-16 year old boys. We cannot demonstrate important differences in the case of cognitive (apperception and assimilation of the insult).

REFERENCES

Berdondini, L., Smith, P.K. (1996): Cohesion and power in the families of children involved in bully/victim problems at school: An Italian replication. *Journal of Family Therapy, 18,* 99-102.

Bowers, K., Smith, P. K., Binney, V. (1994): Perceived family relationships og bullies, victims, and bully/victims in middle childhood. *Journal of Social and Personal Relationships, 11,* 215-232.

Espelage, D. L., Swearer, S. M. (2003): Research on School Bullying and Victimization: What Have We Learned and Where Do We Go From Here? *School Psychology Review. 32,* 365-383.

Farrington, D. P. (1991): Childhood aggression and adult violence: Early precursors and later-life outcomes. In D. J. Pepler, K. H. Rubin (Eds.) *The development and treatment of childhood aggression*. Hilsdale, NJ: Erlbaum, 5-29.

Figula Erika (2004): *Iskolai zaklatás-iskolai erőszak pszichológuszemmel.* Szabolcs-Szatmár-Bereg Megyei Tudományos Közalapítvány Füzetei. 19. Nyíregyháza.

Figula E, Margitics F, Pauwlik Zs. (2019): *The Questionnaire on School Bullying /handbook/.* KeryPub. New York.

Goldstein, A.P. (1994): *The ecology of aggression.* New York, Plenum Press.

Gorman-Smith, D., Tolan P. H., Zelli, A. & Huessmann, L. R. (1996): The relation of family functioning to violence among inner-city minority youth. *Journal of Family Psychology, 10,* 115-129.

Henggeler, S. W., Schoenwald, S. K, Bourdin, C. M., Rowland, M. D., Cunningham, P. B. (1998): *Multisystemic treatment of anti social behavior in children and adolescents.* New York, The Guilford Press.

Loeber, R., Stouthamer-Loeber, M. (1998): Development of juvenile aggression and violence: Some common misconceptions and controversies. *American Psychologist, 53,* 242-259.

Loeber, R., Dishion, T. (1983): Early predictors of male delinquency: A review. *Psychological Bulletin, 94,* 68-99.

Monks, C. P., Smith, P. K., Naylor, P., Barter, C., Ireland, J. R., Coyne, I. (2009): Bullying in different contexts: Commonalities, differences and the role of theory. *Aggression and Violent Behavior, 14,* 146-156.

Nansel, T. R., Overpeck, M., Pilla, R. S., Ruan, W. J., Simons-Morton, B., Scheidt, P. (2001): Bullying behaviors among US youth: Prevalence and association with psychosocial adjustment. *Journal of the American Medical Association, 285,* 2094-2100.

Olweus D. (1980): Familian and temperamental determinants of agressive behavior in adolescent boys: a causal analysis. *Developmental Psychology,* 16. 23-35.

Olweus, D. (1993): Bully/victim problems among school children: Long-term consequences and an effective intervention program. In S. Hodhings (Ed.), *Mental disorder and crime,* (pp. 317- 349). Thousand Oaks, CA: Sage Publications.

Pellegrini, A. D., Bartini, M. (2001): Dominance in early adolescent boys: Affiliative and aggressive dimension and possible functions. *Merrill-Palmer Quarterly, 47,* 142-163.

Révész Gy. (2007): Erőszak az iskolában [Bullying in School]. In. Péley B., Révész Gy.(szerk): *Autonómia és identitás. Tanulmányok Kézdi Balázs 70. születésnapjára.* Pannónia Könyvek, Pécs, 162-179.

Smith, P. K., Madsen, K. C., Moody, K. C. (1999): What causes the age decline in reports of being bullied at school? Toward a developmental analysis of risks of being bullied. *Educational Research, 41,* 267-285.

Thornberry, T. P. (1994): *Violent families and youth violence* (Office of Juvenile Justice and Deliquency Prevention Fact Sheet No. 21). Washington, DC: Department of Justice.

Tolan, P. H., Cromwell, R. E., Braswell, M. (1986): The application of family therapy to juvenile delinquency: A critical review of the literature. *Family process, 15,* 619-649.

Wolke, D., Woods, S., Bloomfield, L., Karstadt, L. (2000): The association between direct and relational bullying and behavior problems among primary school children. *Journal of Child Psychology and Psychiatry, 41,* 989-1002.

<u>Dedication</u>

Thank you, God for carrying me through when I felt weak and couldn't do it on my own. To my husband: you are my rock; you promised your love through sickness and in health, and you meant it. To my sweet children: you were the reason I got up out of that bed every morning and fought that cancer to the ground. You brought laughter and joy into the worst days of my life and gave so many cuddles that helped nurse me back to health. To my parents: I always felt your prayers; thank you for everything. To my siblings: Thank you for your never-ending support. Robin: From stopping by to pray with me after your long work days, to the many text messages of encouragement, I thank you. Natalie: Thank you for organizing meals, visiting, and just being you. You always knew how to keep me laughing! Carrie: God knows when to place someone in your path when we need them most. Thank you for sharing your cancer journey and best of all, your friendship. Keely: You were there since day one of this journey. Thank you, thank you, thank you for your thoroughness in my exam that

And last, but not least, this book is dedicated to those who have fought the good fight and won, the thrivers who fight every day, and the beautiful souls who have moved on from this life, we remember you. To the ones just beginning their journey, my hope is that this book will not only give you insight on what you might expect with treatment, but to let you know that I'm holding your hand through this, cheering you on and I'm praying for you, sweet friend. I will NEVER give up fighting until there is a cure!

day and for handling everything in a timely manner! As always, thank you for being a listening ear when I had many break downs in your office. To me, you truly are a saving grace! Pastor Ed and Janet: Thank you for setting a perfect example of Godly love since I was a little girl. You two played a big role in helping me to grow spiritually. To my In-laws, aunts, uncles, cousins, friends, church family, neighbors, Facebook friends, Pink Sisters and acquaintances: Your prayers and thoughtful words meant more than you'll ever know!

www.ingramcontent.com/pod-product-compliance
Lightning Source LLC
Chambersburg PA
CBHW051236250726
48655CB00006B/2804